POLICY DIALOGUE NO. 13

I0115173

THE ETHIOPIA-ERITREA RAPPROCHEMENT

Peace and Stability in the Horn of Africa

Author
Redie Bereketeab

NORDISKA AFRIKAINSITUTET
The Nordic Africa Institute

UPPSALA 2019

INDEXING TERMS:

Ethiopia
Eritrea
Foreign relations
Regional cooperation
Regional integration
Dispute settlement
Political development
Peacebuilding
Reconciliation

The Ethiopia-Eritrea Rapprochement:
Peace and Stability in the Horn of Africa

Author: Redie Bereketeab

ISBN 978-91-7106-849-1 print
ISBN 978-91-7106-850-7 pdf

© 2019 The author and the Nordic Africa Institute

Layout: Henrik Alfredsson, The Nordic Africa Institute
and Marianne Engblom, Ateljé Idé.

Print on demand: Lightning Source UK Ltd.

Front cover: An Ethiopian mother (R) meets with her daughter from Eritrea
during the reopening border ceremony on September 11, 2018 as two land
border crossings between Ethiopia and Eritrea were reopened for the first
time in 20 years at Zalambessa, nothern Ethiopia. Photo: Stringer / AFP ©

The Nordic Africa Institute conducts independent, policy-relevant research,
provides analysis and informs decision-making, with the aim of advancing
research-based knowledge of contemporary Africa. The institute is jointly
financed by the governments of Finland, Iceland and Sweden.

The opinions expressed in this volume are those of the author and
do not necessarily reflect the views of the Nordic Africa Institute.

Print editions are available for purchase, more information can be found
at the NAI web page www.nai.uu.se.

Contents

Abstract

This book examines the Ethiopia–Eritrea rapprochement and asks whether it might lead to peace and stability in the Horn of Africa. The Algiers Agreement (2000) that was mediated by the international community – the UN, OAU, EU and USA (the same parties that also served as witnesses and guarantors) – was supposed to be final and binding. But when the Eritrea–Ethiopia Boundary Commission (EEBC) published its verdict, Ethiopia rejected it on the grounds that it awarded Badme, the flashpoint of the war, to Eritrea. The witnesses and guarantors, abdicating their responsibility, failed to exert pressure on Ethiopia, which led to a situation of 'no war, no peace'. This stalemate lasted for 16 years, until July 2018. The recent rapprochement is driven by internal dynamics, rather than by external mediation. This has fundamentally reshaped the relationship between the two countries. The impact of the resolution of the Ethiopia–Eritrea conflict goes beyond the borders of the two countries, and has indeed brought fundamental change to the region. Full diplomatic relations have been restored between Eritrea and Somalia; and the leaders of Eritrea and Djibouti have met in Jeddah, Saudi Arabia. This all raises the issue of whether a peace deal driven by internal dynamics fares better than one that is externally mediated. The central question that this book attempts to address is: what factors led to the resolution of a festering conflict? The book explains and analyses the rapprochement, which it argues was made possible by the maturing of objective and subjective conditions in Ethiopia and by the trust factor in Eritrea.

Keywords: Eritrea, Ethiopia, rapprochement, conflict, EEBC, Algiers Agreement

UN HEADQUARTERS, NEW YORK, 28 MAY 1993. Eritrean ambassador Ahmed Haji Ali being directed to his seat in the General Assembly after Eritrea's admittance as a UN member. This image symbolises the international community's recognition of Eritrea after 30 years of liberation struggle. UN Photo / Michos Tzovaras.

OMAN NORWAY

KYRGYZSTA

TREA ~~MATORIAL GUINEA EL SALVAD

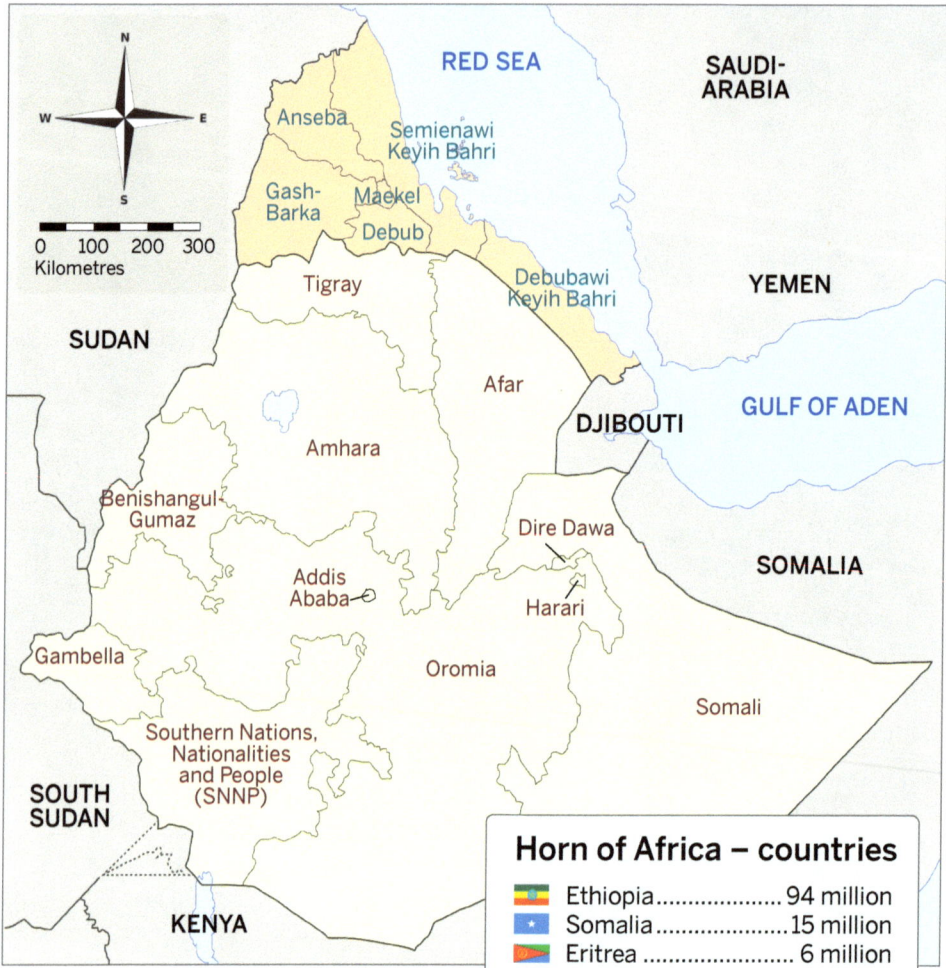

RED SEA

SAUDI-ARABIA

Anseba
Semienawi Keyih Bahri
Gash-Barka
Maekel
Debub
Tigray
Debubawi Keyih Bahri

YEMEN

SUDAN

Afar

GULF OF ADEN

DJIBOUTI

Amhara

Benishangul-Gumaz

Dire Dawa

SOMALIA

Addis Ababa

Harari

Gambella

Oromia

Somali

Southern Nations, Nationalities and People (SNNP)

SOUTH SUDAN

KENYA

N
W E
S

0 100 200 300
Kilometres

Horn of Africa – countries

🇪🇹	Ethiopia	94 million
🇸🇴	Somalia	15 million
🇪🇷	Eritrea	6 million
🇩🇯	Djibouti	1 million
TOTAL		**116 million**

Source: World Bank 2017 (accept for Eritrea and Ethiopia, sources indicated below and left).

Regions of Ethiopia

Oromia	35 467 000
Amhara	21 135 000
SNNP	19 170 000
Somali	5 749 000
Tigray	5 247 000
Addis Ababa	3 434 000
Affar	1 812 000
Benishangul-Gumuz	1 066 000
Dire Dawa	466 000
Gambella	436 000
Harari	246 000
TOTAL	**94 228 000**

Source: Ethiopia Central Statistic Agency, Population Projection 2017

Regions of Eritrea

Debub	1 477 000
Gash-Barka	1 104 000
Maekel	1 053 000
Anseba	894 000
Semienawi Keyih Bahri	897 000
Debubawi Keyih Bahri	398 000
TOTAL	**5 823 000**

Source: National Statistics and Evaluation Office, Eritrea. 2005. Archived from the original on 12 November 2016.

1. Introduction

The 1998–2000 war between Ethiopia and Eritrea ended after international mediation brought about the Algiers Agreement, signed on 12 December 2000 (Algiers Agreement 2000a, 2000b; Fessahatzion 2002; Bereketeab 2009, 2010). A central provision of this Agreement concerned the establishment of the Eritrea–Ethiopia Boundary Commission (EEBC), which was mandated to delineate and demarcate the border between the two countries 'on the basis of pertinent colonial treaties and applicable international laws' (Article 14). The verdict was supposed to be final and binding, and 'The Commission shall not have the power to make decisions ex aequo et bono' (Article 4(2), Algiers Agreement 2000a, 2000b; Bereketeab 2017). As authors of the document, the witnesses and guarantors – the UN, Organization of African Unity (OAU), EU and US – assumed responsibility for ensuring that the decisions of the EEBC would be accepted and implemented unconditionally; and if either or both of the parties reneged on their commitment, the United Nations Security Council (UNSC) would invoke Chapter VII of the UN Charter (Article 14(a)).

The EEBC announced its verdict on 13 April 2002. After an initial expression of acceptance, Ethiopia rejected the ruling, calling it illegal, irresponsible and unjust and demanding renegotiation; meanwhile Eritrea accepted it and called for its unconditional and immediate implementation (Bereketeab 2009). The reason for Ethiopia's rejection was the EEBC's award of the village of Badme, the flashpoint of the war, to Eritrea (Abbink 2003; ICG 2010; Swinkels 2018). Stalemate ensued, compelling the EEBC, in November 2007, to declare the border virtually demarcated and the case legally closed.

Once again, Ethiopia rejected this virtual demarcation, calling it 'legal nonsense'; it insisted on dialogue to resolve the border dispute. Eritrea, meanwhile, held to the view that there was no dispute over the border, since it had been legally delimited and demarcated, and instead there was blatant occupation of sovereign Eritrean territories. This deadlock generated a situation of 'no war, no peace', with occasional serious military clashes between the two armies. This situation persisted for 16 years, until 9 July 2018, when the leaders of the two countries signed an agreement of rapprochement. This rapprochement was sudden and unexpected, and indeed it took the world by surprise – because it came about without the involvement of external mediators. In fact, it came just as some experts and diplomats were urging and advising the guarantors and witnesses to assume (or resume) responsibility and inject life into the dormant peace process (Cohen 2013; Shinn 2014).

Other commentators believed that the parties were not amenable to mediation (Healy and Plaut 2007) and that there was no chance of finding a solution to the festering conflict. This view gained traction when the two countries (plus Sudan) came close to becoming embroiled in another bloody war in January 2018, after a report by Al-Jazeera insinuated that Egypt had deployed soldiers, tanks and combat aircraft in western Eritrea, close to the border with Sudan. This generated frantic military activity, particularly in Sudan. Although the report was never substantiated, Sudan closed its borders with Eritrea and sent thousands of its Rapid Support Force troops to the border, citing a security threat from Eritrea and Egypt (Al-Jazeera 2018). Moreover, reports began spreading that Sudan and Ethiopia were coordinating military activities in eastern Sudan, in Kassala region, on the border with Eritrea. Unconfirmed reports suggested that a battalion of Ethiopian soldiers was stationed in Kassala region and that Ethiopian generals were meeting Sudanese officials in the town of the same name. Eritrea later accused Sudan, Qatar and Ethiopia of supporting Eritrean Islamic terrorist groups (Sudan Tribune 2018). It was amid all this tension that the dramatic and sudden rapprochement occurred. The pertinent question is: why now? What were the factors that made rapprochement possible?

This book examines and analyses the Ethiopian–Eritrean rapprochement. It seeks to answer the central question of what factors contributed to the rapprochement. Along the way, it argues that the maturing of objective and subjective conditions in Ethiopia and the growth of the trust factor in Eritrea facilitated this rapprochement.

The book consists of seven sections. Following this brief introduction, there is a discussion of the sudden and dramatic developments that unfolded. There then follows an analysis of the objective and subjective conditions that matured in Ethiopia, and then an analysis of the growth in the trust factor in Eritrea. The next section discusses the challenges ahead, while the penultimate section analyses the failure of the international mediators to implement an agreement that those selfsame mediators had brokered. The final section offers a conclusion.

"We have seen a conflict, that has lasted for decades, ending, and that has a very important meaning in a world where we see, unfortunately, so many conflicts multiplying, and lasting for ever"

UN Secretary-General António Guterres

2. Dramatic Development that Changed the Political Landscape of a Region

The Secretary General of the UN, Antonio Guterres, described the new development in the region thus: 'There is a powerful wind of hope blowing across the Horn of Africa' (UN News 2018). This wind of hope was unique, in that no one could predict its dynamics, scope or momentum. From a light breeze, it gusted to unprecedented speeds. The vectors of change also multiplied dramatically. And the impact of the conflict between Eritrea and Ethiopia spread beyond the borders of those two countries – indeed, it had far-reaching consequences for the whole region.

Clearly, the Eritrea–Ethiopia conflict formed the epicentre of conflicts in the Horn of Africa. Therefore, its resolution would be a major first step toward addressing the conflicts raging elsewhere in the region (this would subsequently be amply demonstrated by the immediate spread of rapprochement to Somalia, Djibouti, South Sudan and relations between Egypt and Sudan). However, despite a growing realisation of the importance of untangling and unpacking the Eritrea–Ethiopia dispute as a prerequisite for easing the strains and tensions in the region, no serious effort was expended on resolving it. Indeed, it remained a blemish on the behaviour and approach of international mediation. It seemed the general perception was that the conflict was there to stay. As Antonio Guterres noted:

> "We have seen a conflict that has lasted for decades, ending, and that has a very important meaning in a world where we see, unfortunately, so many conflicts multiplying, and lasting for ever." (UN News 2018)

Thus, the sudden and dramatic change came as a surprise to all. Pundits, people of the region, researchers and observers were all unprepared for the dramatic developments. The suddenness and the speed with which the changes occurred took the world by storm. Across the globe, the media focused for days on the Ethiopia–Eritrea rapprochement as a major world event. A state of euphoria engulfed the people of the two countries – a euphoria that was observed during the visits by the leaders of Ethiopia and Eritrea to one another's countries. It demonstrated the stark longing of the people of the two countries for peace and highlighted the importance of the conflict, the urgency of its resolution and the significance of the rapprochement.

On 5 June 2018, the prime minister of Ethiopia, Dr Abiy Ahmed Ali, announced that his government had accepted the EEBC's border ruling and was ready to implement it completely and unconditionally. This announcement also extended an invitation to the Eritrean government to conclude peace and end the state of 'no war, no peace'. The Eritrean government's response came on 20 June, when out of the blue the Eritrean president announced that Eritrea would dispatch a delegation. A few days later, the delegation, led by the minister of foreign affairs, arrived in Addis Ababa.

There followed a reciprocal visit to Eritrea by the Ethiopian prime minister on 8-9 July, amid huge popular rejoicing. On this visit, the two leaders signed a Peace and Friendship Agreement. This Agreement consisted of five points:

1. an end to the state of war,
2. cooperation on political, economic, social, cultural and security issues and the opening of embassies in the respective capitals,
3. links in trade, communication and transport,
4. implementation of the border decision,
5. joint work toward peace and security in the region (Agreement on Peace and Friendship 2018).

The Eritrean president then paid a three-day visit to Ethiopia (14-16 July), in the course of which tens of thousands of Ethiopians lined the streets of Addis Ababa to welcome him and his delegation. The popular exuberance was caught by one commentator:

> "At no point for three decades has peace in the Horn seemed so close. Yet it can sometimes seem as if the region wants peace so much, it has forgotten how recently it was at war". (Yafai 2018).

Thereafter, developments on the region's political landscape snowballed. The Somali president, Mohamed Abdullahi Mohamed, visited Eritrea on 28 July. On 30 July, the two leaders signed a Joint Declaration on Brotherly Relations and Comprehensive Cooperation, consisting of four pillars that would strengthen their relations (Eritrea–Somalia Joint Declaration 2018). Furthermore, the Declaration clearly stated '[respect for] each other's independence, sovereignty and territorial integrity'. The resumption of relations between Somalia and Eritrea just few days after the restoration of those between Ethiopia and Eritrea is a strong indication that the Ethiopia–Eritrea conflict was the primary source of dysfunctional inter-state relations in the region.

On 5-6 September, the leaders of Somalia, Ethiopia and Eritrea held a summit and issued a Joint Declaration on Comprehensive Cooperation Between Ethiopia, Somalia and Eritrea that enhanced their respective territorial integrity, sovereignty and independence (Ethiopia, Somalia, Eritrea Joint Declaration 2018). They also established a Joint High-Level Committee, consisting of the foreign ministers of the three countries. This committee was delegated to visit Djibouti on 6 September and deliver a message from the three leaders to the president of Djibouti. The president of Djibouti welcomed it and voiced his willingness to restore relations with Eritrea – yet another powerful indication of the baleful influence that the Ethiopia–Eritrea conflict had previously exerted in the Horn region.

Pursuant to the Asmara agreements, on 16 September, at the invitation of the king of Saudi Arabia, the president of Eritrea and prime minister of Ethiopia arrived in Jeddah and signed an Agreement of Peace, Friendship and Cooperation in the presence of UN Secretary General Guterres and the king of Saudi Arabia. Thereby, the July Peace and Friendship Agreement gained international status in Jeddah, where the representatives of the UN and the Kingdom of Saudi Arabia formally witnessed it. After the signing ceremony, on 17 September the president of Djibouti came to Saudi Arabia and met his Eritrean counterpart. The meeting was described as historic, although no agreement was announced (beyond an undertaking to restore relations). The significance of the meeting lay in the way it closed the circle: the most estranged states of the region had been able to patch up their relations within a matter of weeks – and most importantly, virtually on their own.

The implementation of the various agreements between Eritrea and Ethiopia gained pace, and on 11 September the leaders of the two countries opened road communications through two border checkpoints. The first was on the south-eastern common border of Debay Sima-Burre, which connects the Eritrean port of Asab and the Ethiopian capital of Addis Ababa. Following the symbolic opening of the road, a hectic round of road repairs got under way, so that traffic could actually commence. The second route was opened along the south-central common border of Serha-Zalambesa region, which connects the capital of Eritrea to Tigray region and on to central and southern Ethiopia. The two leaders flew from the Debay Sima-Burre area to open the Serha-Zalambesa road. The opening of road links was part of the implementation of the provisions of the 9 July Agreement and is intended to facilitate the movement of goods and people. Since these road links opened, there has been a massive movement of people, goods and trucks in both directions.

The importance of the opening of the Serha-Zalambesa road link should be considered from two perspectives. The first is that this part of the common border was highly militarised, with the two countries' armies just a few kilometres apart. Moreover, it is densely populated and the dismantling of the border military posts came as a huge relief to the civilian population living over the border. The second aspect is that the people who live on either side of the border are related by blood, but had been separated, without any contact, for 20 years. Hence the mass dash and the exhilaration once the border was opened. At the same time, they are the people most affected by implementation of the border decision. Therefore, amicable relations between them are important for future peace and stability.

For Ethiopia, one of the major benefits of the rapprochement is the agreements it has been able to negotiate with armed groups in Asmara, Eritrea. The rebel groups controlled tens of thousands of combatants, which constituted a real political and security threat to the government of Ethiopia. But now all the rebel groups have abandoned the armed struggle against the government in Addis Ababa and have returned home to continue their struggle using peaceful means. For Eritrea, the principal gains came in the form of an end to the war, respect for its territorial integrity and sovereignty, and lifting of the sanctions imposed on it nine years ago by the UN Security Council (on 14 November 2018).

To maintain the momentum of the rapprochement and make sure that the agreements are adhered to and implemented, the leaders of Ethiopia, Eritrea and Somalia met for a second summit in the historical town of Bahr Dar, Ethiopia, on 9-10 November. In a joint statement, they 'reaffirmed their commitment to an inclusive regional peace and cooperation' (Joint Statement 2018). They also promised to gather for a third summit in Mogadishu, Somalia.

The agreements concluded between the presidents of Eritrea, Ethiopia and Somalia are presented below in tabular form. All in all, four agreements were signed.

Agreement on Peace and Friendship between Eritrea and Ethiopia

Agreements

The state of war between Ethiopia and Eritrea has come to an end. A new era of peace and friendship has dawned.

The two governments will endeavour to forge intimate political, economic, social, cultural and security cooperation that serves and advances the vital interest of their people.

Transport, trade and communications links between the two countries will resume; diplomatic ties and activities will restart.

The decision on the boundary between the two countries will be implemented.
Both countries will jointly endeavour to ensure regional peace, development and cooperation.

Signed by:
For the State of Eritrea,
Ethiopia,
President Isaias Afwerki

For the Federal Democratic Republic of

Prime Minister Dr Abiy Ahmed Ali

Date and Place:
9 July 2018, Asmara

Eritrea–Somalia Joint Declaration on Brotherly Relations and Comprehensive Cooperation

Agreements

1. Somalia is endowed with a strategic location and vast human and natural resources. However, it has been hampered in realising its potential due to internal problems and external intervention. Thus, Eritrea strongly supports the political independence, sovereignty and territorial integrity of Somalia, as well as the efforts of the people and government of Somalia to restore the country's rightful stature and achieve the lofty aspirations of its people.

2. Somalia and Eritrea will endeavour to forge intimate political, economic, social, cultural, as well as defence and security cooperation.

3. The two countries will establish diplomatic relations and exchange ambassadors, promote bilateral trade and investment, as well as educational and cultural exchanges.

4. Eritrea and Somalia will work in unison to foster regional peace, stability and economic integration

Signed by:
For the state of Eritrea,   For the Federal Republic of Somalia,
President Isaias Afwerki   President Mohamed Abdullahi Mohamed

Date and Place:
30 July 2018, Asmara

Joint Declaration on Comprehensive Cooperation Between Ethiopia, Somalia and Eritrea

Agreements

1. The three countries shall foster comprehensive cooperation that advances the goals of their people.
2. The three countries shall build close political, economic, social, cultural and security ties.
3. The three countries shall work in coordination to promote regional peace and security.
4. The three governments hereby establish a Joint High-Level Committee to coordinate their efforts in the framework of this Joint Declaration.

Signed by:

| For the Federal Democratic Republic of Ethiopia, Prime Minister Dr. Abiy Ahmed Ali | For the Federal Republic of Somalia, President Mohamed Abdullahi Mohamed | For the State of Eritrea President Isaias Afwerki |

Date and Place:
5 September 2018, Asmara

Agreement on Peace, Friendship and Comprehensive Cooperation Between the Federal Democratic Republic of Ethiopia and the State of Eritrea

Agreements

Article One
The state of war between the two countries has ended and a new era of peace, friendship and comprehensive cooperation has started.

Article Two
The two countries will promote comprehensive cooperation in the political, security, defence, economic, trade, investment, cultural and social fields on the basis of complementarity and synergy.

Article Three
The countries will develop Joint Investment Projects, including the establishment of Joint Special Economic Zones.

Article Four
The two countries will implement the Eritrea–Ethiopia Boundary Commission decision.

Article Five
The two counties will promote regional and global peace, security and cooperation.

Article Six
The two countries will combat terrorism as well as trafficking in people, arms and drugs in accordance with international covenants and conventions.

Article Seven
The two countries will establish a High-Level Joint Committee, as well as sub-committees as required, to guide and oversee the implementation of this Agreement.

Signed by:
For the Federal Democratic Republic of Ethiopia,   For the State of Eritrea,
Prime Minister Dr Abiy Ahmed Ali   President Isaias Afwerki

Date and Place:
16 September 2018, Jeddah

> The uprising was initially triggered by a plan to expand the city of Addis Ababa, infringing the land rights of the Oromo people around the capital.

Chapter 3, Page 24

Washington DC, December 2015. Oromo Nationals in a protest rally against the TPLF regime in Ethiopia. Photo credit: flickr/ctj71081.

3. The Maturing of Objective and Subjective Conditions in Ethiopia

It is well known that festering conflicts require the right conditions before they can be resolved. However, it is not always easy to predict when the conditions may be conducive. Neither do the epistemological and methodological tool help us to predict how and when conflicts are ripe for resolution. One thing is clear, however: conflict resolution is predicated on the conditions being right. Conditions may be influenced by external or internal developments, and any attempt to resolve a conflict may prove futile if the conditions are not ripe. This could be why some people advocated allowing the conflict between Eritrea and Ethiopia just to fester; some even suggested letting the two sides fight it out, after which the international community would pick up the pieces. Though cynical, this attitude partly reflected the intractability of the situation. The conflict between Ethiopia and Eritrea that has been festering for the last twenty years is a good example of the dictum that resolution of conflicts are dictated by maturity of underpinning conditions. It was not lack of attempts to resolve the festering conflict, though attempts were feeble, that it has been lingering until now, but the conditions were not yet ripe.

Objective conditions are external to human will and feeling; but those conditions need to be right in order to allow the subjective conditions to mature. Subjective conditions, on the other hand, relate to human will and feeling, and are sufficient for the resolution of conflict because they derive from objective conditions. This sequential relationship between objective and subjective conditions follows the logic that external factors are more easily changed than internal factors. Only when the objective and the subjective conditions are aligned or fulfilled are conflicts ripe for resolution.

The objective conditions necessary to sustain a conflict invariably include economic, political, security, military, diplomatic and other material resources. The total depletion of these resources makes it impossible to sustain a conflict and spawns change in people's mentality or subjective perception – notably a realisation of the need for a change of course. This is what we mean when we talk of the maturing of a subjective condition, which paves the way for a resolution. This maturing of objective and subjective conditions propelled the reform in Ethiopia. So what were the objective and subjective conditions that matured and that enabled the Ethiopia–Eritrea conflict to be resolved?

A popular youth uprising against the ruling party exploded in Oromia in 2015, reflecting deep-seated popular dissatisfaction. The ruling coalition, the Ethiopian People's Revolutionary Democratic Front (EPRDF) consisted of four parties: the Oromo People's Democratic Organisation (OPDO) (now the Oromo Democratic Party or ODP); the Amhara National Democratic Movement (ANDM) (now the Amhara Democratic Party or ADP); the Southern Ethiopian People's Democratic Movement (SEPDM); and the Tigray People's Liberation Front (TPLF) (Markakis 2011; Woodward 2013). Yet for the past 27 years, the TPLF – which represents only 6 per cent of the Ethiopian population – has retained complete domination of Ethiopia's political economy (Milkias 2003).

The uprising was initially triggered by a plan to expand the city of Addis Ababa, infringing the land rights of the Oromo people around the capital. Resistance to the plan quickly developed into political opposition to the ruling party, and in particular the TPLF. The popular uprising constituted a serious threat to the rule of the EPRDF.

In summer 2016, the uprising was joined by young people in the Amhara region (Dinberu 2018). This demonstration of unity by the country's two major – and hitherto antagonistic – ethnic groups constituted a real threat to the survival of the EPRDF, and particularly to TPLF domination. Feeling intimidated, the ruling party resorted to extreme measures: it declared a state of emergency and went on to arrest tens of thousands of civilians, activists, journalists, bloggers and politicians in the hope of containing the unrest. It also blocked the internet. But in spite of the draconian measures, the unrest continued: the young people increasingly targeted economic and industrial institutions supposedly owned by the ruling coalition, and particularly the TPLF.

This hit the economy hard. Investors began to wind up their investments and leave the country; inflation spiralled; and the supply of foreign currency dried up, making it difficult for business. Above all, however, the unrest assumed an ethnic dimension: Tigrayans living outside their own region felt threatened and started to return home. Communal fighting, especially between the Oromo and Somalis, displaced millions of people, and hundreds were killed (Bruton 2018). The crisis also had serious political repercussions: the political tensions and internal divisions both within the ruling coalition and among members of the coalition parties grew (Maru 2018). The political crisis assumed unprecedented proportions and the country was pushed to the brink of collapse. This caused the USA and the EU to send clear diplomatic signals that they were not happy with developments in the country.

This set in motion the maturing of the necessary subjective conditions: the leadership began to realise that unless something was done, the country would drift toward a dangerous disintegration. The steps that were taken were, however, half-hearted, cosmetic and too little: the EPRDF leadership was only ready to undertake minor changes to ensure the domination of the ruling party. Saving the country was associated with saving the EPRDF, since the perception was that there was no ready alternative, should the EPRDF suddenly collapse. The first step taken by Prime Minster Hailemariam Desalegn was to try to reform the political system. But resistance from within the ruling party meant that matters could not proceed at full speed (Schemm 2018; Maru 2018). When the prime minister realised that he would be unable to carry out the desperately needed reforms, he resigned on 15 February. In a statement, he said he had taken the decision 'in order to become part of the solution' and to 'help facilitate the ruling party's reform agenda'. He also admitted that the country was 'at a gravely concerning stage' (Addis Standard 2018). It was clear that PM Desalegn was not the right person to push the fundamental changes required to save the country.

After a power struggle within the EPRDF Council that lasted weeks, in March 2018 Dr Abiy Ahmed Ali of OPDO was elected chairman of the EPRDF, a necessary prerequisite for becoming prime minister. The following month, Abiy was formally elected prime minister. He immediately undertook a range of sweeping measures that included releasing thousands of prisoners, lifting the state of emergency, repealing the terrorism law, sacking senior military and security officers, allowing those websites that had been closed under the state of emergency to reopen, etc.

A general amnesty was declared and all the rebel groups that had been declared terrorists by the previous administration were invited to return to the country and pursue a peaceful political struggle. Accepting the invitation, many armed groups have indeed laid down their weapons and returned, including Patriotic Ginbot 7 (G7), the Oromo Liberation Front (OLF), the Ogaden National Liberation Front (ONLF) and the Tigray People's Democratic Movement (TPDM). Many political activists and opposition groups have also returned from the USA. One of the things that may have convinced many of them is that the prime minister seems to be sincere and genuinely determined to push through the reforms. Unlike his predecessor, he possesses the necessary characteristics to succeed. His admission in a televised address to the House of Representatives that the EPRDF government had committed crimes was sensational.

This admission came in response to those members of the House who opposed the general amnesty on the grounds that the opposition had committed crimes. The prime minister's admission, coming as it did from someone who is part of the system, exploded like a bombshell. The TPLF was furious, but the move indicated the prime minister's earnestness to reform the system, and that reassured the Ethiopian people. Moreover, the galvanising concepts of love, conciliation, compromise, forgiveness, inclusivity and an overarching 'Ethiopianness' that the prime minister used in his speeches were well received both inside and outside the country. The revivalist national ideal that imbued Ethiopians with self-respect, pride and long-lost glory rekindled the spirit in most Ethiopians that Ethiopia is a great nation. The overarching Ethiopianness is designed to tackle the ongoing drift toward the country's disintegration into its component elements that led to the reforms, and is a sort of social contract.

It is also the case that the majority of Ethiopians associate the crimes committed over the years with the TPLF, which has now been dethroned; and therefore PM Ahmed is widely perceived to be untainted. Indeed, many Ethiopians wish to see the TPLF banned (Walle 2018). Those who regard ethnic federalism as a dangerous scheme that will tear apart Ethiopian society (Balcha 2008), and who hold the TPLF responsible for it, are demanding the removal of ethno-nationalism and the TPLF itself (Dinberu 2018). The TPLF is no longer in the driving seat. It has moved onto the back foot, adopting a hostile stance toward the changes and becoming very conservative, defending the status quo ante. It promotes itself as the defender of the constitution, national institutions, the rule of law and the old system – a position at odds with that of the overwhelming majority of Ethiopians.

The acceptance of the EEBC decision on the border and the invitation for Eritrea to engage in a move toward peace are well thought-out and decisive elements in the reform process. PM Ahmed knew that unless the conflict with Eritrea was resolved, the reforms in Ethiopia would be incomplete. The only way of resolving a conflict that had been allowed to fester for 16 years was to unconditionally and completely accept and implement the border decision that followed the Algiers Agreement – something that his predecessors had failed to do. On 5 June, the prime minister announced that his government would unconditionally accept and implement the border decision. He then extended the hand of friendship to the Eritrean government, inviting it to respond positively so that the two governments could improve relations and work for peace, stability and development. And indeed, the Eritrean government did respond positively.

"

The Ethiopian govern-
ment expected Eritrea
simply to collapse like
a pack of cards.

Chapter 4, Page 29

The Tank Graveyard in Asmara, Eritrea. A collection of scrapped military equipment and other vehicles, a reminiscent of Eritrea's fight for independence. Photo Clay Gilliland, May 2016.

4. The Trust Factor: Eritrea

In an interview, the former prime minister of Ethiopia, Hailemariam Desalegn, claimed that what Abiy Ahmed had offered Eritrea was no different from what he and his predecessors had offered – and which Eritrea had consistently rejected. He went on to say that the difference was that the times had changed.

Desalegn may truly believe that his offer of peace through implementation of the Algiers Agreement border verdict was genuine. But powerful forces were not genuine in their peace offer – or at least that was the Eritrean perception. Desalegn was never taken seriously on matters as important as the border issue: the common perception was that it was the TPLF that wielded the real power, and it was not prepared to cede Badme.

The trust between the TPLF-dominated EPRDF government and the People's Front for Democracy and Justice government in Eritrea hit rock bottom following the outbreak of war in 1998. Both governments were convinced that the problem could only be resolved if the other one vanished, and therefore they both did all in their power to depose the other, actively supporting opposition groups (Abbink 2003; Lyon 2009). The EPRDF government even tried to destroy the Eritrean state, resorting to economic, diplomatic, political and international campaigns to completely isolate Eritrea (Mengisteab 2014).

Following the end of the 1998–2000 war, the TPLF strategy shifted to economic strangulation. The Ethiopian government expected Eritrea simply to collapse like a pack of cards. The assumption was that an isolated and economically bankrupt Eritrea would sink under the weight of popular political discontent. When this economic pressure failed to provoke popular resentment and the collapse of the state, all manner of dubious ploys were devised to get the UN to impose sanctions on Eritrea (Bereketeab 2013). These included unsubstantiated allegations of support for the extremist Al-Shebab group and fabrication of an attempt to bomb an African Union summit meeting; border dispute with Djibouti; allegations that Eritrea was undermining peace in the region; and more recently claims of human rights violations – all designed to completely isolate Eritrea. The Intergovernmental Authority on Development (IGAD) was also drafted in and was instrumental in initiating the demand for imposing the sanctions endorsed by the UN Security Council in 2009 (Mengisteab 2014). Later, when Eritrea tried to activate its membership of IGAD after an absence of several years, the move was blocked by Ethiopia (Andemariam 2015; Bereketeab 2018). For its part, Eritrea effectively utilised the Ethiopian rebels based in Eritrea to counter Ethiopia's ill intentions (Lyon 2009). Indeed, the tens of thousands of rebels may have served to deter Ethiopia from any military adventures. Since, it would also mean fighting Ethiopians alongside Eritreans who were located along the common border.

Clearly, given the absolute lack of trust, there was no possibility of settling the conflict. Any attempt by one side was perceived as malicious deception intended to outmanoeuvre the other, rather than as a genuine gesture designed to resolve the conflict.

The election of Dr Abiy Ahmed Ali fundamentally changed the rules of the game.

For Eritrea, it brought about a radical change in power relations in Ethiopia in two dimensions. First, there was a geographical shift, from the north to the south, away from Eritrea's borders. Secondly, power shifted from the TPLF (representing the people of Tigray) to OPDO (representing the Oromo people). The shift meant a reconfiguration of Ethiopian–Eritrean relations generally, and the Ethiopia–Eritrea conflict in particular. The transition of power goes beyond a simple personality change or change of party colours. There has been a sea change: for the first time in recent history, the Eritrean issue in Ethiopian politics is being handled outside the Abyssinian establishment. No longer are relations with Eritrea under the control of the TPLF, which always reckoned that the Eritrean issue should serve the interests of Tigray. During the TPLF's struggle against the Dergue (Ethiopia's military regime) – and particularly when it dreamt of creating a Republic of Tigray – it viewed its survival as intimately connected with Eritrea (Bereketeab 2009, 2010). The Ethiopian statesman Meles Zenawi, in a 1990 interview with Paul Henze, put it this way:

> We look at this from the viewpoint of the interest of Tigray, first, and then Ethiopia as a whole. We would like to see Eritrea continuing to have a relationship with Ethiopia. We know that Tigray needs access to the sea and the only way is through Eritrea. Whether Eritrea is part of Ethiopia or independent, we need this access and, therefore, must have close ties. There are many Tigrayans in Eritrea. They are concerned. They don't want to be treated as foreigners there. There has always been close connections between Tigray and Eritrea for the highland people are all the same. They have the same history. (Ethiopia 2012:9)

Also, following the independence of Eritrea and the ascendance of the TPLF to state power in Ethiopia, Eritrea was perceived as a backbone of TPLF domination in Ethiopia. In spite of the widespread perception that Meles unequivocally supported Eritrea's independence, this is his 1990 (who was then chairman of the EPRDF) response to Paul Henze's question: 'But we really hope that Eritrea can remain part of a federated Ethiopia' (Ethiopia 2012:9). The TPLF is a minority in the EPRDF and the people of Tigray constitute only 6 per cent of the total population of Ethiopia: this makes it very difficult for the party to sustain its domination of Ethiopian politics indefinitely. It became imperative to tie the Eritrean issue to the party's survival as a dominant force.

To this end it promised the Ethiopian people that it would deliver the thing they valued most: access to the sea (Fessahatzion 1999). During the 1998–2000 Ethiopia–Eritrea war, in an attempt to mobilise the population and portray the party as the protector of Ethiopian interests, TPLF officials promised to deliver the Eritrean port of Asab to the Ethiopian people. Some commentators even claim that the objective of the military was to capture Asab: 'The military ... was victorious but came back grudgingly when Meles stopped it short of its goal: the occupation of Asab' (Milkias 2003:52).

The fact is, however, that after Meles announced (at the end of May 2000) that the war was over, there were about 10 failed attempts by the Ethiopian army to capture Asab before the Ceasefire Agreement was signed in Algiers on 18 June. The previous president of Tigray region, Mr Gebru Asrat, has openly advocated reclaiming Asab (Asrat 2014). Meles, in a 2006 interview with local media, said that his government had agreed to 85 per cent of the border verdict; however, on the remaining 15 per cent, Ethiopia would never concede. It was widely assumed that this referred to the village of Badme (a concession that the current leadership of the Tigray regional state also opposes).

What may further complicate the issue of Badme is that it is caught up in a larger territorial claim within Ethiopia itself: when the military regime was defeated and the TPLF-dominated EPRDF captured state power, it carried out a controversial regional reconfiguration. This meant that the Tigray region expanded, thanks to the inclusion of the territories of Raya from Wollo region and Welqait from Gonder region. Badme was caught up in this. When the power of the TPLF began to wane, voices in Raya and Welqait began to question the legality of their incorporation into the Tigray region; now there are demands for the territories to be given back to the old regions. Just as the TPLF rejected the surrender of Badme to Eritrea, so it also rejects reinstating Raya and Welqait. The return of Badme could have implications for the future of those regions, too.

As far as Eritrea is concerned, the side-lining of the TPLF therefore ushered in a new perspective on relations. There are two dimensions to the new Eritrea–Ethiopia relationship (and to the confidence that Eritrea has derived from it). The first concerns the Eritrean leadership, and particularly the president; the second concerns the Eritrean people.

With regard to the Eritrean leadership, the shift of power has confirmed two things: first, the Eritrean president could claim to have been vindicated in his stated assessment of 'game over' for the TPLF in Ethiopia; and secondly, he could also claim to have won, while the TPLF has lost. For 20 years, the TPLF tried to depose his government; but now instead it has lost power. He can now engage with the new Ethiopian leadership, which he believes is to be trusted. No more is Eritrea the political domain of the TPLF.

There seems to be a good chemistry between the president of Eritrea and the prime minister of Ethiopia. The Eritrean president has visited Ethiopia several times, including Addis Ababa, Hawasa and Amhara region, and the leaders of many of the regional states of Ethiopia have been to Eritrea. However, the Eritrean president has not been to Tigray, and the leader of Tigray has not visited Eritrea.

With regard to the Eritrean people, the shift of power is also a victory. There is a feeling among Eritreans that, for the first time in 27 years, Ethiopians might have genuinely accepted the independence of Eritrea. The Agreement of 9 July 2018 reiterated respect for its independence, territorial integrity and sovereignty (Agreement on Peace and Friendship 2018). This replaced the common view that it was a conspiracy between the Eritrean People's Liberation Front (EPLF) and the TPLF that led to the illegal separation of Eritrea (cf. Milkias 2003). The presentation of a camel (a symbol of the Eritrean liberation struggle) to the Eritrean president during his visit to Ethiopia and commemoration of Nakfa (an icon of Eritrean perseverance and resilience) were clear indications of the recognition of Eritrean sovereignty. The emergence of a government that does not automatically include Eritrea in the Ethiopian power equation is seen as some assurance to the Eritrean people.

Moreover, Eritrea has – for the third time – played a major role in political change in Ethiopia. The first time was in the demise of the emperor in 1974; the second was in the collapse of the Dergue regime in 1991; and in 2018 came the downfall of the TPLF as the omnipresent and omnipotent power. In a deeper sense, from a social-psychological point of view the shift of power to the Oromos resonates with the deep-seated, embedded perception of victimhood. Eritrea can identify better with an underdog that has been on the receiving end of Abyssinian injustice. The feeling is that the Oromo 'victim' will be more understanding and less aggressive. This could explain the exhilaration of the Eritreans, tens of thousands of whom turned out in the streets of Asmara to welcome the prime minister of Ethiopia on 8 July 2018. That level of jubilation was last witnessed in May 1991, when Eritrea was liberated. Many have described the events of 2018 as a second liberation.

Thus, the shift of power in Ethiopia has profoundly affected Ethiopia–Eritrea relations. Eritrea's trust of the new Ethiopian leadership was boosted, and that spurred the Eritrean leadership to jump at the Ethiopian invitation. It took many by surprise when the president, on 20 June, announced that he would send a delegation to Ethiopia to explore, at first hand, the seriousness of Ethiopia's offer to accept the border decision. The speed at which events moved subsequently provides some indication of the trust that had built up.

> There must be a clear understanding of what is meant by assertions such as 'we are one people' or 'the border has no meaning'.

Chapter 5, Page 39

January 14, 2019. Ethiopian Prime Minister Abiy Ahmed Ali meets with David Mabuza, Deputy President of South Africa and Special Envoy to South Sudan. Photo: GCIS

5. Challenges Ahead

Undoubtedly, the rapprochement will face numerous challenges. One could come from within Ethiopia; another could stem from the relations between Ethiopia and Eritrea. With regard to the first challenge, Ethiopia needs to tackle its internal unrest. In spite of the change of leadership, the unrest has continued under the new prime minister, too. There are several reasons for this. First, the young people who spearheaded the protests wanted to see immediate change in many areas. In this respect, it seems they are not sure how far the new prime minister is willing and able to push reform; thus keeping the pressure up is one way of ensuring steady progress. As the reform has unfolded, so additional challenges – visible and invisible – have arisen.

Second, those forces that are losing power because of the changes are determined to put up a last-ditch resistance, and it seems that they are provoking and exploiting inter-ethnic cleavages. One example is the Somali-Oromo intercommunal unrest that is widely believed to have been instigated by the Special Forces (liyu hail) supporting the president of the Somali region (Woldie 2018). Another is the unrest persisting in the Oromo and Benishangul-Gumuz regions. The disarming of the OLF combatants who have returned from Eritrea has also become something of a hot potato for the Oromo regional state. It seems the OLF leadership wants to make sure that the combatants are properly integrated before committing itself to disarming. According to one informant, they want to avoid any repetition of what happened to the Oromo soldiers when the EPRDF came to power in 1991. Then, Oromo soldiers of the Dergue were demobilised, leading to the domination of the TPLF. Recently, a military and political deal was struck between the OLF and the regional government of Oromia to include integration of the OLF combatants into the military and security forces.

The third challenge concerns the security and military forces. Bringing these forces under the political control of the new prime minister has proved a real problem. The reason is that the two institutions – the military and the security forces – were under the control of the TPLF, where the uppermost level of the power structure was dominated by ethnic Tigrayans; transferring loyalty to a new power holder – particularly if that person comes from a different ethnic group – will be difficult until those senior officers come to terms with the 'change of guard' (or are replaced by others who are loyal to the new authorities). In recognition of this challenge, the prime minister immediately enforced change in the leadership of the security and military forces, retiring senior officers, including the army chief of staff, General Samora Yunis, and the director of the National Intelligence and Security Service (Zelalem 2018). The 16 June attempt on the life of the prime minister was believed to be associated with forces unhappy with the reform, and the previous chief of intelligence was allegedly implicated. The prime minister has taken a series of bold and potentially risky measures to transform the military, and is reported to have said that 'the major work of his government since he took power seven months ago was undertaking major reform in the army'. The satellite news outlet Ethsat reported on 10 November that 160 generals had been retired (Ethsat, 2018). Reform of the army is still continuing: on 13 December 2018, it was reported that the command posts had been reduced from six to four, in an effort to reflect loyalty to the constitution and ethnic representation (Borkena 2018).

In its 13 November issue, Walta Media reported:

> About 36 of the suspects are employees of the National Intelligence and Security Service (NISS), who have been arrested on allegations of human rights violations, including beatings, torture, sodomy, rape, electrocution and killings. The remaining 28 are from the state-owned Metals and Engineering Corporation (METEC), including Brigadier General Tena Kurdin, who have been detained on allegation of serious corruption. (Walta Media 2018)

This was followed by the arrest of the former head of METEC, Major General Kinfe Dagnew. The arrest of the senior officials has provoked a strong reaction from the regional government of Tigray. The deputy president of Tigray region, Dr Debretsion Gebremichael, in an interview with local media on 19 November, claimed that 'the pretext of corruption and human rights violation are being used to attack Tigrayans'.

The fourth – and main – challenge, of course, came from the TPLF, which makes up the government of Tigray region. The TPLF, which controlled Ethiopia for 27 years as the dominant partner in the ruling coalition, found itself relegated to a minor role. This impelled it to openly challenge the reforms, alleging that they are taking place in violation of the constitution and are not based on national institutions (Maru 2018). It launched a campaign under the slogan of protecting and defending the constitution and national institutions, which are in jeopardy. In a thinly veiled threat, the deputy president of Tigray region told a public gathering in Mekele, capital of the region, on 28 July 'we either respect each other or disintegrate'. Many interpreted this as a signal that the TPLF could invoke Chapter 39 of the constitution, which provides the right to secede.

The tension between the federal government and the regional government is increasingly becoming a constitutional challenge. The TPLF's charge of constitutional and institutional violation by the federal government is tantamount to a charge of illegality against the federal government. The tension has grown following the arrest of people suspected of corruption and human rights violations: the TPLF sees this as targeting Tigrayans. The regional TPLF government regards the continuation of the unrest as evidence of the unfolding chaos in Ethiopia, saying it is the outcome of lawlessness, violation of the constitution and dislocation of national institutions (Maru 2018). The TPLF has accused the new government of incompetence and inability to run the country. The ongoing demonstrations in Tigray are seen as a strategy devised by the TPLF to mobilise the people of Tigray in preparation for any eventuality.

The security situation in the Somali region briefly got out of hand and required the intervention of the federal army. There, too, the TPLF regional government accused the federal government of violating the constitution by sending the federal army into the region. The second TPLF bone of contention concerned the rapprochement between Ethiopia and Eritrea (Ethiomedia 2018). It stuck to its old position that the border issue could only be resolved through negotiations between the local populations affected by the border demarcation (Viral News 2018), ignoring the fact that international borders are decided by nation states. A demonstration throughout Tigray was officially called in support of the Ethiopia-Eritrea Peace and Friendship Agreement, but in reality was turned into an opposition demonstration against the reforms in Ethiopia: there was not a single mention of the Algiers border decision by the demonstrators and leaders of the TPLF who addressed the demonstrators.

It would seem that it is to give the TPLF time to come on board that both governments have opted to delay implementation of the fifth point in the Peace and Friendship Agreement – the border issue. According to a federal government official, if the Eritreans can wait for 30 years, it will not hurt to wait for a few more months; at the end of the day, it is the federal government that decides. Although the demarcation occurred in November 2007, the TPLF rejection stood in the way of implementation; now that the federal government has conceded acceptance, the matter of the occupation by and withdrawal of the army poses practical problems. The matter of the present residents of Badme also need to be resolved. The challenge is formidable, so long as the TPLF continues to reject implementation of the border decision. In the last week of September 2018, the four coalition parties of the EPRDF convened separate gatherings in the run-up to the EPRDF's 11th Congress. While three of the parties introduced fundamental changes to their programmes, policy and leadership (even changing names), the TPLF demonstrated no inclination to introduce any meaningful change. This signals that it wants to continue with its confrontational attitude. In addition, it demonstrates a clear ideological split among the coalition parties: while the TPLF adheres to revolutionary democracy, the others are steadily moving toward liberal democracy (Walle 2018). By sticking to its ideology, the TPLF is not only lagging behind, but is also deliberately distancing itself from, the other coalition members.

A serious crack has opened up in the unity of the EPRDF (Maru 2018). At its centre lies the legacy of Meles Zenawi, the strongman of the TPLF. While the TPLF still valorises him, wants to preserve his legacy and has a strong desire for the EPRDF to be guided by his vision, the other coalition members are rapidly abandoning him, banishing from public spaces any symbols that recall him: reportedly, his photograph has been removed from the building of the House of Representatives. The fifth anniversary of his death was marked by an absence of key figures from the EPRDF leadership, including the prime minister.

It seems only a matter of time before the EPRDF splits. But so long as the issue remains unresolved – either with internal unity or the parties going their separate ways – the ruling coalition will remain unstable. This constitutes a challenge to the rapprochement between Ethiopia and Eritrea in the long run, as well as to regional peace and stability.

Recently, a serious dispute erupted between Amhara regional state and Tigray regional state. The dispute primarily concerns two regions – Welqait and Raya – which the TPLF incorporated into its regional state, but which now Amhara region is claiming back. The conflict has increasingly assumed a dimension that goes beyond territorial claims and that could be described as having become a symptom of a deep-seated mistrust between the people of Amhara and Tigray. Indeed, the deputy president of Tigray's belligerent statements and threats against unspecified enemies that were 'defeated before' is a worrying sign.

It is doubtful whether the EPRDF will run as a united coalition in the next election, scheduled for 2020. Observers are convinced that a split is inevitable; the question is whether it occurs before or after the election. The tensions and fractures among the coalition parties and the challenges emanating from other regional political parties are serious enough for many observers to conclude that the EPRDF will not survive an election. If it collapses, the question is what will happen to the rapprochement.

Another challenge to the rapprochement could be the differences in economic policy between the two states, Eritrea and Ethiopia. In the documents they have signed so far, they have expressed their ambition of economic integration. In the Agreement on Peace, Friendship and Comprehensive Cooperation, Article Three states "The two countries will develop Joint Investment Projects, including the establishment of Joint Special Economic Zones". The major obstacle to economic integration between the two countries is the huge imbalance in the size of their economies, which comes in addition to the huge demographic asymmetry. For the last 20 years, Eritrea's economy has suffered badly, while Ethiopia's economy has undergone an immense transformation. This asymmetry could gradually strain economic relations.

Already, some Eritreans are expressing the fear that Eritrea might be swallowed up by the neighbouring economic and demographic giant. Eritrea may end up as a dumping ground for Ethiopian products, which could well hamper its economic recovery. This fear and sense of insecurity, coupled with other developments, both foreseen and unforeseen, could easily derail what is generally a positive start. It is, therefore, imperative that economic plans, policies, strategies, logics and rationalities are constructed in a way that manages the asymmetries.

A further major challenge concerns ideology. As matters stand today, the two countries will certainly face veritable ideological differences. There are clear indications that the Ethiopian government is pursuing a neoliberal economic policy of privatising key state-owned economic institutions and industrial establishments, such as Ethiopian Airlines, and providing unimpeded open access to transnational capital – thus risking a further widening of the already large gulf between the (few) rich and the (many) poor. In all his speeches, the prime minister emphasises the individual economic rights of Ethiopians. Meanwhile, the Eritrean government is guided by a national liberation ideology, which prioritises the collective interest, the equitable distribution of resources, and an economic policy based on justice and equality that bridges the gap between the rural and urban populations (Government of Eritrea 1994; EPLF 1994). It further adheres to collective ownership of key economic resources.

These are two ideological orientations that the governments need to reconcile. In practice, when they begin implementing economic agreements, they will indeed encounter huge challenges. Political liberalisation in Ethiopia will also constrain the relationship:

that trend in Ethiopia needs sooner or later to be matched by some kind of political libe-ralisation in Eritrea. It will need institutions, regulations, laws, regimes and conven-tions that correspond to those in Ethiopia, if the relationship is to function smoothly. Harmonising trade relations will constitute a real challenge. Although differences in economic policy between independent states should not (and in this case did not) cause war, they can lead to a rupture in diplomacy. Many Ethiopians are convinced that the different economic policies were the main factor in the outbreak of the 1998–2000 war (Tadesse 1999; Abbay 2001), though no evidence – either theoretical or empirical – is offered of this. Nevertheless, for a healthy and enduring relationship to prevail, it is imperative to harmonise trade relations.

When it comes to Eritrea, the challenges also concern how to deal with the inter-nal situation. The Eritrean government has rationalised the state of the country as being due to the conflict with Ethiopia. According to it, the state of 'no war, no peace', the sanctions and the policy of isolation threatened the very existence of Eritrea, and therefore its government was compelled to introduce practices and norms that are far from 'normal'.

Many problems of national importance were shelved. Now that the conflict has been resolved, the government needs urgently to address those domestic issues, the most prominent of which include national service, prisons and inmates, the national constitution, national elections, activating the legislative body, etc. In addition issues of reviving the economy, improving the infrastructure, housing, employment, the salary system, water and electricity supply, and a revival of the private sector all require prompt attention. If they do not receive it, the outflow of young people will probably not be stemmed; the implications of that could affect relations between the two countries.

Many people warn that the two governments need to tread very carefully to avoid going back down the road of the post-independence experience. One reason why their post-independence relationship collapsed is that it was based on individual leaders, rather than being anchored in institutions and in open and transparent principles and guidelines. In order to avoid repeating the same mistakes, the current agreements need to be applied by focusing on national institutions (legislative, judiciary), popular aware-ness and participation, as well as principles of transparency, accountability, jurisdic-tion and conventions. Personality-based relations contributed to the disastrous war of 1998–2000. Any illusions concerning the nature and scope of the relationship should be exposed: there must be a clear understanding of what is meant by assertions such as 'we are one people' or 'the border has no meaning', and by phrases such as 'integration and unity', 'reconciliation', etc. Most of the time, these have different meanings for Eritreans and Ethiopians. It is important to dispel any misconceptions about Eritrean sovereignty and to underscore its irreversibility. There are still many Ethiopians who would like to see Eritrea through the lens of ports and an outlet to the sea. Hence, it has to be made clear that the foundation of the partnership is the mutual sovereignty of the two states. It is to be recalled, once before, great promise turned into nightmare (Tekle 1994; Fessahatzion 2002).

Aerial view of the Mereb Bridge on 7 July 2001, the day of the reopening ceremonies Ethiopia and Eritrea. Photo Jorge Aramb, UN Photo.

6. The Failure of International Mediation

The Algiers Agreement was mediated by a cluster of international actors: UN, OAU, EU, USA (Algiers Agreement 2000). The document signed by the warring parties was authored by those four as representatives of the international community. In addition, they promised to be the guarantors and witnesses of the agreement, which was supposed to be final and binding. By agreeing to this, they committed themselves to shouldering the legal, political and moral responsibility for ensuring that the agreement was implemented in full and unconditionally.

The guarantors and witnesses, however, reneged on this commitment and responsibility. When the Eritrea–Ethiopia Boundary Commission announced its verdict on 13 April 2002 (Zondi and Rejouis 2006), the response from the parties did not reflect the commitment they had made in December 2000: when it realised that Eritrea had been awarded the village of Badme, the flashpoint of the war, Ethiopia rejected the commission's findings (Healy and Plaut 2007; Lyon 2009; ICG 2010). Although primary responsibility for implementation lay with the warring parties, the guarantors and witnesses bore great responsibility. They should have intervened to tell Ethiopia in no uncertain terms that if it failed to honour its commitment, they would refer the matter to the UNSC, which would invoke Chapter VII of the UN Charter, as per the Algiers Agreement. Instead, however, the witnesses and guarantors engaged in appeasement.

By failing to take a strong position against Ethiopia, the guarantors and witnesses contributed to the 'no war, no peace' situation that lasted until 9 July 2018. Indirectly, they became complicit in the human suffering and economic disaster of the two countries. A conflict that had already claimed the lives of tens of thousands of soldiers was allowed to fester and inflict further immense human suffering, material destruction and waste (Bereketeab 2009). As a matter of principle, mediators are obliged to remain neutral, if they are to fulfil their solemn duty.

Moreover, it was an International Court of Arbitration verdict that was wilfully ignored, which seriously undermined the international court of arbitration regime and – by extension –tainted the integrity and credibility of the body. This opens the way to other aggrieved states simply to ignore international court of arbitration verdicts. If mediators do not respect their commitments, what is the point of international mediation? What is the point of the so-called international community, with its international laws, conventions, agreements and commitments? These are questions that we seriously need to ponder.

The Eritrea–Ethiopia case provides a clear indication of how geo-strategic interest dictates international mediation and law. US officials of both the Bush and the Obama administrations sought actively to alter the binding and final nature of the EEBC verdict. They openly advocated the renegotiation of the border decision, in line with the Ethiopian demand. In 2006, US Assistant Secretary of State for African Affairs Jendayi Frazer, for instance, visited the village of Badme (under the control of Ethiopia) and suggested holding a referendum so that the people of the village could decide on its future; this was in contravention of the Algiers Agreement (Woldemariam and Yohannes 2007; Lyon 2009). Susan Rice (US ambassador to the UN at the time) was also instrumental in imposing sanctions on Eritrea in what was widely perceived as an attempt to undermine the border verdict. These acts were in blatant violation of the Algiers Agreement. Furthermore, Frazer instructed the US ambassador to the UN, John Bolton, to reopen the 2002 EEBC decision (Bolton 2007).

In his book Surrender is Not an Option, Bolton notes:

> I certainly had not favorite, but it seemed to me that Eritrea had a point. Ethiopia had agreed on a mechanism to resolve the border dispute in 2000 and was now welching on the deal … it was time to terminate UNMEE, which simply propping up Ethiopia's flat violation of its commitments … I said we should solve the problem and not let it fester, France, Japan and several other Council members agreed with me … For reasons I never understood, however, Frazer reversed course, and asked in early February to reopen the 2002 EEBC decision, which she had concluded was wrong, and award a major piece of disputed territory to Ethiopia. I was at loss how to explain that to the Security Council. (Bolton 2007: 344–348)

The USA's push for the renegotiation of the EEBC verdict was driven by the importance Ethiopia had for its policy in the region: Ethiopia is a powerhouse of the region, as well as a vital ally of the USA's in maintaining the latter's geo-strategic interest, and particularly its global war on terror (Woodward 2013; Mengisteab 2014). Ethiopia proved its usefulness in the global war on terror by invading Somalia and serving as policeman for the Horn of Africa (Samatar 2013; Möller 2013). Eritrea, on the other hand, was a nuisance for US policy in the region. The strategic location of the Horn of Africa compels the US to seek a permanent presence in the region, either physically or by proxy – a role in which Ethiopia has been a reliable actor throughout the post-colonial, Cold War and post-Cold War eras (Woodward 2006; Schemm 2018; Schmidt 2013; Yordanov 2016). This necessitated pursuing a distorted mediation process that conformed to geo-strategic interests and politics.

Geo-strategic interests and alliances are based on realpolitik or realism, which usually upholds the pragmatic power balance, unlike idealism (which strives for justice, equality and dignity for all). Based on this doctrinal preference it became imperative for the US to side with Ethiopia, at the expense of international law. This had dire consequences for Eritrea in particular, and for the Horn of Africa generally. The abdication by the witnesses and guarantors of the responsibility they had shouldered testifies to the dictates of realpolitik. But the injustice did not stop with the disregard exhibited for the International Court of Arbitration verdict: it was extended to the imposition of sanctions on the basis of unsubstantiated evidence. This led to Eritrea losing all confidence in the Western powers, and this severely affected its diplomatic relations with the West. The blind support given by the West – and particularly the USA – to the regime in Addis Ababa also infuriated Ethiopians, who similarly began to doubt the Western commitment to democracy and human rights in their country.

The abdication of mediation responsibility permitted non-Western actors to step in to facilitate the current rapprochement between Eritrea and Ethiopia (ICG 2018). Although the rapprochement seems to have been internally driven, the Kingdom of Saudi Arabia and the United Arab Emirates played an important role in the facilitation and successful conclusion of the rapprochement. One lesson that could be drawn from the rapprochement is that an internally driven conflict-settlement and peacebuilding effort is much more durable than one that is externally driven. Furthermore, the Eritrea–Ethiopia rapprochement lends credence to the mantra of "an African solution to African problems", as advocated by the African Union.

7. Concluding Remarks

This book set out to analyse the rapprochement between Ethiopia and Eritrea. Following two years of bloody war (1998–2000) and 16 years of 'no war, no peace' – when the armies of the two countries were condemned to live in trenches, watching one another, and the borders of the countries were completely sealed – everything changed in July 2018. Suddenly, the leaders of the two countries were sitting together, discussing how to resolve their differences and normalise relations. This came as a great surprise. The rapprochement enjoyed wide-ranging commendation both for its role in resolving one of the most vicious and protracted conflicts in Africa, and because of the implications for the intricate and festering conflicts in the Horn of Africa, as well as across the Red Sea and the Gulf region. The suddenness with which the changes took place caught observers unawares. It also indicates two things. The first is the eagerness of the people of the two countries to see peace between them. They had been longing for the moment, and when it came they embraced it wholeheartedly. This was observed in the jubilation expressed during the visits by the national leaders to one another's countries. The second thing it shows is that the objective and subjective conditions were ripe for a settlement. And that is what is required: goodwill may not be enough. The Eritrea–Ethiopia conflict is proof of that.

The suddenness and rapidity of the change caused many to wonder why and how rapprochement could occur now, at this time and at this pace. There were two factors whose fulfilment made rapprochement possible: on the one hand, the objective and subjective conditions; on the other hand – trust. In endeavouring to analyse and interpret developments and answer the 'why' question, we have employed here two explanatory and analytical conceptual categories: the maturity of objective and subjective conditions; and the trust factor. Whereas the maturity of objective and subjective conditions refers to Ethiopia, the trust condition refers to Eritrea.

The central argument of this book is that it was the alignment of these two elements that rendered rapprochement possible. The book has argued that the economic, political and security crises that erupted in Ethiopia following the popular uprising – primarily in the most populous regions of Oromia and Amhara – pushed Ethiopia to the brink of collapse. The popular uprising was the culmination of decades of general resentment, economic marginalisation, ethnic discrimination, corruption, human rights violations, suppression and maladministration. The youth had derived little benefit from the impressive economic growth of the last decade and a half. The EPRDF government took a series of draconian measures to contain the uprising, which led to further gross human rights violations. When every attempt to suppress the youth uprising failed, it increasingly became clear that the time had come for a controlled change of leadership and political course. But that did not satisfy the youth, and therefore the uprising continued, forcing Prime Minister Hailemariam Desalegn to resign. A new leadership was installed, confirming the maturity and consummation of both the objective and subjective conditions. The new leadership embarked on fundamental politico-economic reforms. Moreover, it realised that unless the Ethiopia–Eritrea conflict was resolved, the reforms would be incomplete. It thus issued a peace call to Eritrea that was received positively.

The change in leadership brought a profound shift in power across both the geographical and the ethnic dimension. The locus of power moved from north to south, and from Tigrayans to the Oromo. This profound shift of the power centre in turn spurred Eritrea's confidence that it could do business with the new leadership. The maturing of the objective and subjective conditions in Ethiopia, coupled with greater trust in Eritrea, heralded the sudden and rapid rapprochement.

Cooperation between states is never free of friction. And certainly, the Ethiopia–Eritrea rapprochement will face serious tests, as detailed in this article. Regional cooperation and integration are presumed to be successful if they are based on certain common values and norms. They also presuppose some kind of symmetry between partners. A major hurdle that the countries need to face is the huge demographic and economic asymmetry. Unless they find some formula to address this, it could disrupt the functioning and sustainability of the relationship. Expectations and hopes also need to reflect realities in both countries and in the region as a whole. Peace, stability and development will become a reality only if the problems of the region are addressed in a holistic way, adopting approaches and mechanisms that reflect the commonalities and complementarities of the region.

Some of the basic common values and norms that are necessary prerequisites for conflict settlement and peace building and that can lead to well-functioning and sustainable regional integration and cooperation include ideological, cultural, political, governance and economic systems. Some of these already exist. The region is well known for being imbued with commonalities, in terms of history, culture, topography, mode of life, demography and ethnicity. These are some of the features that the governments could capitalise on. Using these infrastructures as the base, the leaders of the region need to construct a superstructure that can support successful and enduring integration and cooperation. This would cover ideology, political governance, economic systems, civic and social rights. The rapprochement between Eritrea and Ethiopia – as well as in the region as a whole – therefore requires the adoption of some basic common norms and values, embodied in common general ideology that guides economic, political, social, security and governance policies and strategies. It is imperative for the leaders of the region to engage in earnest, to negotiate and to hold dialogue on such issues. They also need to involve technocrats, professionals, intellectuals and experts in identifying elements, formulating, designing and building a strategy, and transforming it all into a programmatic roadmap. If the distance to be traversed in this is too great, the success of the integration may be short lived. But Eritrea and Ethiopia, to say nothing of the region as a whole, possess many commonalities that could easily bind the region together. The experience of Eritrea and Ethiopia between 1993 and 1997 should serve as a profound lesson.

A reformed IGAD, as the regional organisation, could take the lead in identifying, cultivating and linking the commonalities of values and norms. As a regional economic community (REC), it is well placed to pursue the process of integration, peace building and development. Moreover, as one of the RECs acknowledged by the African Union as component units of the continental organisation, IGAD is actually mandated to advance the integration process. In this, it would get a helping hand from the continental and international organisations. Therefore, to avoid the Eritrea-Ethiopia rapprochement being reversed and to serve the goals of peace, stability, development and integration in the region and beyond, it needs to be incorporated into the greater project of the RECs – in this case IGAD. The Ultimate test of the rapprochement lies in whether it will bring peace, stability and development to the region.

References

Abbay, Alemseged. 2001. *Not with them, not without them: The staggering of Eritrea to Nation-hood*, Africa, vol. LVI, no. 4, pp. 459–491

Abbink, Jon. 2003. *Ethiopia-Eritrea: Proxy wars and prospects of peace in the Horn of Africa'* Journal of Contemporary African Studies, vol. 21, no. 3, pp. 407–425

Addis Standard. 2018. *Breaking: Ethiopia PM Hailemariam Desalegn resigns*, 15 February 2018

Agreement on Peace and Friendship. 2018. 9 July, Asmara, Eritrea

Agreement on Peace, Friendship and Comprehensive Cooperation between the Federal Democratic Republic of Ethiopia and the State of Eritrea. 2018. 16 September, Jeddah, Saudi Arabia

Algiers Agreement. 2000a. Agreement on Cessation of Hostilities Between Ethiopia and Eritrea. Organization of African Unity, 18 June

Algiers Agreement. 2000b. Agreement between the Government of State of Eritrea and Government of Federal Democratic Republic of Ethiopia. Algiers

Al-Jazeera. 2018. *Sudan deploys more troops to Eritrea borders: Khartoum says it is facing 'threat' from its eastern border as tension in the Red Sea region continues to rise*, 5 January

Andemariam, Senai W. 2015. *In, out or at the gate? The predicament on Eritrea's membership and participation status in IGAD'*, Journal of African Law, vol. 59, no. 2, pp. 1–25

Asrat, Gebru. 2014. *Sovereignty and Democracy in Ethiopia*. Gaithersburg: Signature Book Printing Press

Balcha, Berhanu Gutema. 2008. *Ethnicity and restructuring of the state in Ethiopia*, DIIPER Research Series, Working Paper no. 6. ISSN: 1902-8679

Bereketeab, Redie. 2009. *The Eritrea-Ethiopia conflict and the Algiers Agreement: Eritrea's road to isolation*, in Richard Reid (ed.), Eritrea's External Relations: Understanding its regional roles and foreign policy. London: Royal Institute of International Affairs

Bereketeab, Redie. 2010. *The complex roots of the second Eritrea-Ethiopia war: Re-examining the causes*, African Journal of International Affairs, vol. 13, nos 1&2, pp. 15–39

Bereketeab, Redie. 2013. *The morality of the UN Security Council sanctions against Eritrea: Defensibility, political objectives, and consequences*, African Studies Review, vol. 56, no. 2, pp. 145–161

Bereketeab, Redie. 2017. *The role of the international community in the Eritrean refugee crisis*, Geopolitics, History, and International Relations, vol. 9, no. l, pp. 68–82

Bereketeab, Redie. 2018. *The intergovernmental authority on development: Internal culture of foreign policymaking and sources of weaknesses*, in Jason Warner and Timothy M. Shaw (eds), African Foreign Policies in International Institutions. New York: Palgrave Macmillan

Bolton, John. 2007. *Surrender is Not an Option: Defending America at the United Nations*. New York: Simon and Schuster

Borkena. 2018. *Defense force downsized number of command posts*, 13 December. https://borkena.com/2018/12/13/defense-force-downsized-number-of-command-post (accessed 14-12-2018)

Bruton, Bronwyn. 2018. *Ethiopia: End game?*, Atlantic Council, 14 February

Cohen, Hank. 2013. *Time to bring Eritrea in from the cold*, African Arguments, 16 December

Dinberu, Tefera. 2018. *Ethnic nationalism must be replaced by Ethiopian nationalism*, ZeHabesha.com, 10 October

EPLF. 1994. *A National Charter for Eritrea: For a democratic, just and prosperous future.* Approved by the Third Congress of the Eritrean People's Liberation Front (EPLF), Nacfa, February

Eritrea-Somalia Joint Declaration. 2018. *Eritrea-Somalia Joint Declaration on Brotherly Relations and Comprehensive Cooperation*, Asmara, 30 July

Ethiomedia. 2018. *Ethiopians reject government peace offer to Eritrea*, 19 July. https://ethio-media.com/2018/07/19/ethiopians-reject-government-peace-offer-to-eritrea/ (accessed 09-10-2018)

Ethiopia. 2012. *Meles Zenawi's interview with Paul Henze 1990*. https://tassew.wordpress.com/2012/06/17/meles-zenawis-interview-with-paul-henze-1990/ (accessed 09-10-2018)

Ethiopia, Somalia, Eritrea Joint Declaration. 2018. *Joint Declaration on Comprehensive Cooperation Between Ethiopia, Somalia and Eritrea*, Asmara, 5 September

Ethsat. 2018. '*Over 160 generals fired from the Ethiopian army*, 10 November

Fessahatzion, Tekie. 1999. *Explaining the unexplainable: The Eritrea-Ethiopia border war*, Eritrean Studies Review, vol. 3, no. 2

Fessahatzion, Tekie. 2002. *Shattered Illusions, Broken Promises: Essays on the Eritrea-Ethiopia conflict, 1998–2000*. Trenton: Red Sea Press

Government of Eritrea. 1994. *Macropolicy Document.* Asmara: Government Press

Healy, Sally and Martin Plaut. 2007. *Ethiopia and Eritrea: Allergic to persuasion*, Africa Programme Briefing Paper. London: Chatham House

ICG. 2010. *Eritrea: The siege state*, African Report no. 163, 21 September

ICG. 2018. *The United Arab Emirates in the Horn of Africa*, Crisis Group Middle East Briefing No. 65

Joint Statement. 2018. *Joint Statement of the Bahr Dar Meeting Between the Leaders of Ethiopia, Somalia and Eritrea*, Bahr Dar, 10 November

Lyon, Terrence. 2009. *The Ethiopia-Eritrea conflict and the search for peace in the Horn of Africa*, Review of African Political Economy, vol. 36, no. 120, pp. 167–180

Markakis, John. 2011. *Ethiopia: The last two frontiers*. Woodbridge and Rochester: James Currey

Maru, Mehari Taddele. 2018. *The Old EPRDF is Dead, Cant its System be Saved? Five Steps to Save the Federation*, Ethiopian Insight. https://www.ethiopia-insight.com/2018/10/03/the-old-eprdf-is-dead-can-its -system-be... accessed 29-01-2018

Mengisteab, Kidane. 2014. *The Horn of Africa*. Cambridge and Malden: Polity Press

Milkias, Paulos. 2003. *Ethiopia, the TPLF, and the roots of the 2001 political tremor*, Northeast African Studies, vol. 10, no. 2, pp. 13–66

Möller, Björn. 2013. *Militia and piracy in the Horn of Africa: External responses*, in Redie Bereketeab (ed.), *The Horn of Africa: Intra-state and inter-state conflicts and security*. London: Pluto Press

Samatar, Abdi Ismail. 2013. *The production of Somali conflict and the role of internal and external actors*, in Redie Bereketeab (ed.), *The Horn of Africa: Intra-state and inter-state conflicts and security*. London: Pluto Press

Schemm. Paul. 2018. *Ethiopia's Prime Minister Hailemariam Desalegn resigns amid political turmoil*, Washington Post, 15 February

Shinn, David. 2014. *Time to bring Eritrea in from the cold (but it's harder that it sounds)*, African Arguments, 13 January

Schmidt, Elizabeth. 2013. *Foreign Intervention in Africa: From the Cold War to the War on Terror*. Cambridge, New York, Melbourne, Madrid, Cape Town, Singapore, Sao Paulo, Delhi, Mexico City: Cambridge University Press

Sudan Tribune. 2018. *Eritrea renews accusations to Sudan, Ethiopia, Qatar of supporting Jihadist groups*, 16 May

Swinkels, Jules. 2018. *Twenty years after Ethiopia-Eritrea war: Rapprochement and reflection*, Horn Institute. https://horninstitute.org/twenty-years-after-ethiopias-and-eritreas-point-less-war-rapprochement-and-reflecting-after-20-years/ (accessed 04-10-2018)

Tadesse, Medhanie. 1999. *The Eritrean-Ethiopian War: Retrospect and prospect.* Reflections on the making of conflicts on the Horn of Africa, 1991–1998. Addis Ababa: Mega Printing Enterprise

Tekle, Amare (ed.). 1994. *Eritrea and Ethiopia: From conflict to cooperation.* Trenton: Red Sea Press

UN News. 2018. *"Wind of hope" blowing through Horn of Africa says UN chief, as Ethiopia and Eritrea sign historic peace accord*, 16 September. https://news.un.org/en/story/2018/09/1019482 (accessed 20-01-2019)

Viral News. *Ethiopia and Eritrea's second rapprochement*, 19 September. https://newsviralzone.com/ethiopia-and-eritreas-second-rapprochement/ (accessed 04-10-2018)

Walle, Tadesse. 2018. *Call for TPLF to ban itself, the alternative is unsustainable, at best indefensible and mockery of justice*, ZeHabesha.com, 6 October

Walta Media. 2018. *Rights violations, corruption suspects appear before court*, 14 November. http://www.waltainfo.com/news/editors_pick/detail?cid=43698 (accessed 15-11-2018)

Woldemariam, Yohannes and Okbazghi Yohannes. 2007. *War clouds in the Horn of Africa*, Sudan Tribune, 12 November

Index

About the Policy Dialogue Series

The Nordic Africa Institute Policy Dialogue Series is intended for strategists, analysts and decision-makers in foreign policy, aid and development. It aims to inform decision-making and the public debate.

The Policy Dialogue publications are generally written by researchers and based on their original research, but can also include contributions from experts and analysts with a perspective from outside the academic world. The opinions expressed are those of the authors and do not necessarily reflect the views of the Institute.

The series aims to offer a deepened understanding of a current topic, with an explicit purpose of giving policy relevant advice.

A list of previous titles in the Policy Dialogue Series can be found below:

1. HAVNEVIK, K., BRYCESON, D., BIRGE-GÅRD, L.-E., MATONDI, P., & BEYENE, A. (2007). African Agriculture and The World Bank : Development or Impoverishment?

2. ZACK-WILLIAMS, A., & CHERU, F. (2008). The quest for sustainable development and peace : the 2007 Sierra Leone elections.

3. UTAS, M., PERSSON, M., & COULTER, C. (2008). Young female fighters in African wars : conflict and its consequences.

4. UTAS, M. (2009). Sexual abuse survivors and the complex of traditional healing : (G)local prospects in the aftermath of an African war.

5. ERIKSSON BAAZ, M., & STERN, M. (2011). La complexité de la violence : Analyse critique des violences sexuelles en République Démocratique du Congo (RDC).

6. VOGIAZIDES, L. (2012). 'Legal Empowerment of the Poor' versus 'Right to the City' : Implications for access to housing in urban Africa.

7. VAINIO, A. (2012). Market-based and Rights-based Approaches to the Informal Economy : A comparative analysis of the policy implications.

8. ERIKSSON BAAZ, M., & UTAS, M. (Eds.). (2012). Beyond "Gender and Stir" : Reflections on gender and SSR in the aftermath of African conflicts.

9. GELOT, L., & DE CONING, C. (Eds.). (2012). Supporting African peace operations.

10. NLANDU MAYAMBA MBUYA, T. (2013). Building a Police Force 'for the good' in DR Congo : Questions that still haunt reformers and reform beneficiaries.

11. FOLLÉR, M.-L., HAUG, C., KNUTSSON, B., & THÖRN, H. (2013). Who is responsible? : Donor-civil society partnerships and the case of hiv/aids work.

12. ADETULA, V. A. O., BEREKETEAB, R., & JAIYEBO, O. (2016). Regional economic communities and peacebuilding in Africa : the experiences of ECOWAS and IGAD.

OPEN ACCESS

All titles can be downloaded in full text for open access.

Please visit NAI's online research publication database DiVA at http://nai.diva-portal.org.

www.ingramcontent.com/pod-product-compliance
Lightning Source LLC
Chambersburg PA
CBHW060843270326
41933CB00003B/180

9 789171 068491